UNFORGIVENESS

Kenneth Hagin Jr.

Chapter 1
FORGIVE AND FORGET

And Jesus answering saith unto them, Have faith in God.

For verily I say unto you, That whosoever shall say unto this mountain, Be thou removed, and be thou cast into the sea; and shall not doubt in his heart, but shall believe that those things which he saith shall come to pass; he shall have whatsoever he saith.

2

Therefore I say unto you, What things soever ye desire, when ye pray, believe that ye receive them, and ye shall have them.
— Mark 11:22-24

People get all excited about these three verses. The verses tell us what we can get from God, what God can do for us, and how we can use our faith to receive.

Nearly everybody stops reading with Mark 11:24, but this discourse which the Master started in verse 22, describing what I call "possibility faith," doesn't end with verse 24!

In the following verses, Jesus makes two more statements that are vitally important for faith. The first is in verse 25:

MARK 11:25
25 And WHEN YE STAND PRAYING, FORGIVE, if ye have ought against any; that your Father also which is in heaven may forgive you your trespasses.

Jesus ties this thought to verse 24 with a conjunction. If this had been edited correctly in King James' time, there would not be a period after "them" in verse 24; there would be a comma and then the word "and" joining the two thoughts. These two verses were meant to go together.

Most people stop reading at the end of verse 24 and get all excited about receiving the things they desire. Too many Christians live in this kind of whoopee-type world instead of the real world. Believers need to get their feet on the ground in order to get something done for themselves and the rest of the kingdom.

Notice in verse 25 that the Father calls holding grudges against our fellow man "trespasses." This is serious. When you study the various translations, you can see *you need to forgive so your Father can forgive you of your sins.* Really, it is a sin to hold grudges against people.

People say, "Well, I can *forgive,* but I'll never *forget* what they've done to me." That's not forgiving. I once heard a man say, "I know I have to forgive in order for

God to meet my needs. I tell you what, I'm going to forgive them, but I'm never going to forget what they did to me.''

You have to let it drop, forget it, no matter what someone's done to you. *The Amplified Bible* says, ''And whenever you stand praying, if you have anything against any one, forgive him and let it drop.''

''Yeah, but you don't know what they did to me,'' some will protest.

Have they killed you yet? Have they hung you on a cross yet? Jesus said, ''Father, forgive them, because they don't understand what they're doing.''

When somebody says something about you that you don't like, you say, ''I'm not going to let them get away with that! They're not going to make *me* look like a fool and get away with it!'' Then, out of the other side of your mouth, you say, ''Oh, thank God, I'm confessing that God will meet all of my needs.''

How in the world can God meet your

needs when you're not living in line with God's Word? Look at what He says in verse 26:

MARK 11:26
26 But if ye do not forgive, neither will your Father which is in heaven forgive your trespasses.

The Lord is not talking to sinners here; He's talking to believers — those who have the God-kind of faith. Sinners don't have the God-kind of faith. Only those who have been born again have received the God-kind of faith. Every believer has a measure of it. Every believer can make it grow by exercising it and feeding it on God's Word. This God-kind of faith is of the heart, not the head. But it will not work where there is unforgiveness.

No, we don't like to hear these kinds of things taught. We want to live the way *we* want to live and enjoy everything the way *we* want to enjoy it. We don't want to come in line with the real truth of God's Word.

The Apostle Paul warned in Second Timothy 4:3 that the day would come when people would heap to themselves teachers who would teach what the people wanted to hear because they had "itching ears."

As I wrote in my minibook *Itching Ears,* it's time you realized there are a lot of other doctrines in the Word of God besides faith and healing.

I know people who would walk out of the church if the preacher got up and started teaching on a topic like unforgiveness. They would say, "Bless God, I'm not going to listen to anything but *faith!*" They won't endure sound doctrine.

Feeding on only one part of the Word will do you harm. You need a balanced diet for your spiritual man just like you do for your natural man.

When I was a youngster in elementary school, our teachers showed us drawings of a fellow who ate candy, ice cream, and other junk food all the time. He started out big and strong, but after a while, he became weak and wasted. Our teachers were trying to teach us the fact that if we ate just one kind of food, we'd either become weak, wasted, or fat.

The same is true with "eating" or feasting on the Word of God. If you don't eat a balanced diet, you will become imbalanced. And do you know what happens to imbalanced people? Most of the time they go "off the deep end."

By using simple logic, we could save ourselves a lot of problems, but for some reason, when some people get saved and filled with the Holy Spirit, they throw all their natural knowledge out the window.

I make the following statement all the time at RHEMA: *The natural and the supernatural working together become an explosive force for God.* Either one by itself can't really do the job; it takes both working together.

Chapter 2
WHY PRAYERS AREN'T ANSWERED

Unforgiveness is the reason why many people do not get answers to their prayers. Oh, they can quote the Scriptures; they can make all the right confessions; they can give you the 25 steps to faith — but all of a sudden, faith is not working in their life.

I have counseled such people. They say, "I just don't understand it. My faith won't work. I can't understand what's going on."

I start asking questions to try to find out something about them. I find they know the Word. They can quote it. Then I begin to check up in some other areas. I begin to ask them about their lifestyle to find out if they're living in any kind of open sin we would consider not in line with God's Word. I ascertain that they're living a good, clean life.

Then I say, "All right, since all these

other areas are clear, there's only one area left: the area of forgiveness and walking in love. Has anybody done anything that you think they shouldn't have done to you?"

"Well, it's funny you should ask that," a RHEMA student once replied. "About two months ago, my roommate decided he wanted to move out. We had made a pact to live together for the entire school year, but he decided he wanted to live by himself.

"I could not afford to keep our apartment — it was really nice — and I had to move into a 'dump.' I just don't like it, because he didn't hold up his end of the bargain. He did me wrong!"

I said, "What do you mean, he did you wrong? Didn't he give you notice?"

"Oh, yes, he told me two months before the lease ran out on the apartment — but still we had agreed to live together for the entire school year."

I said, "But he stayed the length of

time you signed the lease for, and besides that, he gave you two months' notice."

"I don't care. That wasn't right. He didn't do me right. I had to move to another place, and it's too far from school and a lot of other things."

I said, "I want to tell you something, fellow. You'd better forget about it right now. If you don't, you're going to get in trouble in every area of your life."

He replied, "Well, I'm going to tell *you* something — I'm *not* going to forget the way he treated me. He treated me like dirt!"

I said, "Hey, man, back off."

He said, "Oh, no."

We had to expel that young man from RHEMA with less than a month of the school year to go. Because he got upset with his roommate and wouldn't forgive him, he gave the devil a place. He began to rebel against the rules, saying, "I don't see why they've got that rule. I don't have to obey that. I don't believe that's in line with God's Word.''

Because we're training people for the ministry, we like the men to wear dress slacks and regular shirts, not jeans and T-shirts, to school. This fellow started coming to school wearing jeans and T-shirts. He'd argue, ''Well, I don't see why I can't wear jeans and T-shirts. I'm free.''

The faculty member who dealt with him said, ''The main reason you can't wear them is because that's one of the rules that's been established at RHEMA.''

He said, ''But I don't find that in the Bible.''

The faculty member said, ''I don't find in the Bible where it says you've got to have a driver's license to drive, either, but you go out and try to drive without one. Get stopped by a policeman and see what happens to you.''

At the beginning of the school year, this young man had been a very good student who showed great promise. Then, by holding that grudge, he allowed unforgiveness into his heart.

What happened to him? The devil got him completely confused, hoodwinked, and all messed up. He went completely "off the deep end," rebelling against everything — and it all started with unforgiveness.

Do you know what happens when you start holding grudges? It's the same thing that happens in the arteries of your heart when too much fat gets in. Fat starts collecting around the edges of the artery and restricting the flow of blood. Once it starts collecting, it builds up and builds up until no blood can flow at all.

In the spiritual realm, unforgiveness builds up the same way. It starts collecting in the channel where the Spirit flows, and if you're not careful, it'll clog the channel. Soon nothing is flowing at all.

Get on your knees before God, take the knife of the Holy Spirit, and cut out all that unforgiveness. When you get rid of it, the flow can start again.

You see, it says in God's Word, *"And when ye stand praying, forgive."* Of course, you don't always have to go to the individual. Sometimes I have gone to an individual to settle a matter because I felt it was necessary. Other times, when I stand praying, the Lord brings it to my remembrance that someone has wronged me and I have not forgiven them. So I simply say, "Lord, I forgive that person. I ask you now to forgive me for harboring a grudge against them."

I refuse to dwell on evil things that somebody says to me — and I've had plenty of opportunity, raised in a preacher's home, to hold everything against everybody! When you're a teenager and you hear people talking against your father and his stand on the Word, you've got every opportunity to get upset — or even get in a fight!

I remember the time a bunch of us preachers' kids were up in the balcony during a convention. Some of the other boys started saying more than I thought they should, and we got into a scuffle. I was only about 14 at the time.

Later on, when I really began to get serious with God, I asked the fellow I had fought with to forgive me. "I shouldn't have done that," I said. "That wasn't right. I want you to forgive me."

He said, "No way! You whipped me. I'll hold it against you till the day you die."

I said, "That's your problem, not mine. I've done what God told me to do. I love you, man."

That fellow's not even living for God today, and I attribute part of it to his holding grudges, because once you start trespassing (holding grudges) in one area and give the devil one inch of ground, he'll start to take you over in other areas, and he'll push you into a corner.

Now, as I said, I do get upset. Anybody with any gumption gets upset occasionally, but the Word of God says, *"Be ye angry, and sin not: let not the sun go*

*down upon your wrath: Neither give place
to the devil"* (Eph. 4:26,27).

There's a difference between getting
upset and holding a grudge. I didn't say
you couldn't disagree with somebody. But
did you know you can disagree *agreeably?*
There are certain things in the Word of
God that allow room for differences of opi-
nions, and no one is going to see eye-to-eye
with us on everything. We can disagree on
certain issues.

However, I'm not going to hold a
grudge against someone because he
doesn't believe the same way I do. If he
believes in being saved by the blood of the
Lord Jesus Christ, that's what counts. If
he truly believes in salvation and tries to
live in line with God's Word, that's
grounds enough for me to fellowship with
him.

A lot of you won't even fellowship with
people like that. You say, "Bless God, if
they don't believe it all the way, I'm not
going to be around them."

How in the world are you ever going to get them to see the truth of God's Word if you refuse to talk with them?

Some of you are going to be surprised at the people you'll find in heaven. The only prerequisite for getting to heaven is being born again by the blood of the Lord Jesus Christ. They don't have to believe in healing; they don't have to believe in prosperity; and they don't have to speak in tongues! In heaven you will fellowship with people you ignored down here because they didn't believe exactly as you did.

I've heard pastors say, "Bless God, I wouldn't join that ministerial alliance — too many unbelievers there." The pastoral staff of RHEMA Bible Church are very active in our local ministerial alliance. Even when I was pastoring years ago in another state, I was involved in the ministerial alliance. At that time years ago, I knew some men in the group probably weren't saved, but the majority were.

One day we all sat around a table and talked about how God had called each of us into the ministry. I was really surprised to hear what some of the Methodist and Baptist ministers had to say. They told about being out in the woods praying for several hours when God spoke to them about getting into the ministry. I thought only Pentecostals did that!

Chapter 3
FORGIVENESS IN THE CHURCH

Most charismatic churches are made up of people who have come out of denominational churches, and many of you are holding grudges against your former denomination. As soon as someone mentions your former church, you bristle, "Bless God, they did me wrong. They taught unbelief. They had no right to kick me out. I didn't do anything wrong!"

Even if they did you wrong or taught you wrong, you can't hold a grudge if you expect God to use you. Let that be between God and them. Do not let yourself be cut off from the flow of God's presence by holding a grudge or giving a bad report.

Many churches have problems because people in the congregation hold grudges against each other. They sit out there in the congregation, thinking they have been wronged and, without realizing it, play into the devil's hands.

They keep the power of God from being able to move effectively among the whole body of believers because they're thinking, *I can sing better than that! I don't know why the pastor put her up there to lead worship. I have a better voice. Listen to that! She went flat on that note.*

Or, *I wish the pastor would shut up. He's been preaching 35 minutes. He already said that three times — what's he saying it again for?*

Or, *I taught that Sunday School class last year. The pastor should have chosen me! I'm better qualified!*

If you're not careful, this kind of thing will build up resentment in you, and before you know it, you won't want to go to church.

Instead of getting upset and acting in unforgiveness, speaking an evil report, you should give a good report. You should say, "Well, praise God, the pastor must know what he's doing."

You should go to that person chosen to

teach your former class and say, "I taught this class last year. I have a lot of notes and research you're welcome to use if you would like."

That's acting in love. That's the way it should be, because then the enemy will have no room to get in. Then the power of God can move. Then your words won't snare you:

PROVERBS 6:2
2 Thou art snared with the words of thy mouth, thou art taken with the words of thy mouth.

The Book of James has a lot to say about this. James talks about the wagging tongue. He talks about having faith. And he wonders how your faith is going to work if that tongue is always wagging.

(That's what's the matter with a lot of people. God couldn't move if He wanted to because they're never quiet long enough for Him to say anything to them.)

Words are filled with something. They are containers. They are either filled with hate, doubt, and unbelief, or they are filled with love, joy, peace, faith, and goodness. You build an atmosphere with words.

It's the same in the spiritual realm: *Forgive and keep a good report.* Let whatever flows out of your mouth be good!

If you have all the "formulas" right, but your prayers are not getting answered, the first thing to do is check to see if you're holding a grudge against somebody. There's nothing wrong with the power end (God), so the problem must be on the receiving end (you).

If you're tuning in a radio station and the signal's garbled, you don't call the radio station and say, "Hey, your signal's no good; you need to check the transmitter."

It's not the fault of the transmitter; something's wrong with your radio. You have to do something. Either the tuner's not working properly, or you're too far away from the signal to pull it in with the type of antenna you have.

So when your faith's not working for you, you'd better start fine-tuning at your end of the line.

Never permit anything said about you to remain in your memory. If you think on those barbs long enough, they will begin to affect you. The devil will jump on your shoulder and say, "If I were *you*, I'd wait for an opportunity to get back at them!"

Many people have trouble like this on their jobs. They may feel they've been wronged or passed over for promotions, so they try to get even with the person they believe wronged them. When they see that person making a mistake, they make sure the mistake is noticed by everybody.

That's harboring unforgiveness to the point where you begin to sin against your fellow man.

The other day as I was walking across the RHEMA campus, a young man came up to me and said, "I want you to forgive me."

I said, "What for?"

He said, "Don't you remember? The other day we were over at the recreation center and I said such and such."

I said, "No, I don't remember."

He said, "I do."

I said, "Well, now that you've started bringing it up, maybe you did. But I never hold anything against anybody. Yes, I forgive you. Go on."

I make it a rule if somebody says something to forgive them that very moment, and I never even think of it again.

GALATIANS 6:1
1 **Brethren, if a man be overtaken in a fault, ye which are spiritual, restore such an one in the spirit of meekness; considering thyself, lest thou also be tempted.**

Many people get into trouble when they see somebody doing something *they* think is wrong (whether it is or not). They may say something like, "My goodness, I can't believe it! Look what he's doing. I don't believe that's right."

Even if it *is* wrong, Paul didn't say, "People, if a man be overtaken in a fault, you who are spiritual get on the telephone and tell everybody about it."

Paul didn't tell you to say, "Do you know what I saw So-and-so doing? That isn't right. We ought to do something about that. We ought to go tell the pastor. We ought to bring it up before the church. We ought to expose him." That's holding ought against your brother.

No, the Bible says, "*Ye which are spiritual, restore such an one in the spirit of meekness; considering thyself, lest thou also be tempted.*"

When you stand praying, forgive those who have done wrong to you or others. Do not allow unforgiveness to get hold of you. I didn't say it would be easy, because sometimes it's not easy to forgive or forget.

Whenever I have trouble forgiving, I go back in my mind to Jerusalem, to Golgotha, a place by a garden outside the city walls. Many believe that is where Jesus hung on the cross.

I remember the words He uttered as He was dying. He was stretched between heaven and earth, the bridge on which man passes from sin to eternal life. He said, "Father, forgive them."

If the Son of God can forgive like that, I can forgive, too! When I find it hard to forgive and forget, I remember that Jesus forgave — and it becomes quite easy.

Nobody has put a crown of thorns on my head. Nobody has beaten my back bloody. Nobody has put me to death. If Jesus can forgive, so can I. All I've had to endure is a little tongue-lashing.

The Holy Spirit will help you forgive. *The Amplified Bible* quotes Jesus in John 14:16 as saying, "And I will ask the Father, and He will give you another Comforter (Counselor, Helper, Intercessor, Advocate, Strengthener and Standby) that He may remain with you forever."

The Holy Spirit is a Helper. He is with

you. If you choose to forgive and forget and to keep a good report, the Holy Spirit will help you. But until *you* choose to forgive, the Holy Spirit cannot help you. Oh, He wants to help!

He wants to place a hand, as it were, over your mouth and say, "Don't say that! Don't think about that! Don't say that evil! Don't listen to that!" But the choice is yours.

It's your choice to speak faith words — loving words — and not say anything evil. *You* control what comes out of your mouth. You can choose to talk about how badly you feel, how bad economic conditions are, or how badly somebody acted toward you.

You can choose to talk about those in authority and bad-mouth them all day long, dwelling on their bad points, but if you dwell on these kinds of things, they will become a giant and eat you alive.

On the other hand, you can choose to talk about God and how great He is. You can choose to say good things about people who have wronged you. You can choose to talk about the goodness of God, how great it is to be alive, and what a wonderful day God has made.

It's your choice to hold a grudge or forgive.

It's your choice to speak faith words (positive words) or failure words (negative words).

I personally choose to be positive and keep a good report coming out of my mouth. I refuse to hold ought against anybody. If somebody wrongs me, I forget it — I let it go — and I pray for them.

Chapter 4
TRUE FORGIVENESS

Paul said in his writings, "Faith worketh by love." Love isn't bothered by trivial things. Love overlooks them. Love forgives them. Love lets them go.

When you truly love somebody, you forget their failings and mistakes. That's what the Word says God does with us. It says that He forgives us of our sins and He forgets them — it's as if we never had sinned.

When most people see their children doing something they don't like, they correct them, but they don't hold that mistake against them every time they make another. But there are some people who dangle a previous mistake in front of the child, saying, "Remember what you did last week?" Once you've corrected a problem and dealt with it, forget it and go on. Don't bring it back and hammer the child over the head with it.

A lot of you do that when it comes to forgiving someone. You say you forgive them, and you let them back into fellowship, but if that person steps out of line the least bit, you grab them and say, "Hey, remember what you did before? This is the second time I've had to talk to you about it." How much forgiveness is in that?

Some people hinder their own prayers by reminding God of their past. He's forgotten it — He's forgiven you — so don't remind Him of it.

You see, *true forgiveness is acting like it never happened.* That's true love: never thinking about it.

If you want to be strong in faith, you've got to be strong in love and forgiveness; especially in forgiveness. I realize this is not an "exciting" teaching — it doesn't make you want to jump over benches — but it will give you a foundation that will stand in the midst of the storms.

I know that most of you already have all those verses in the 11th chapter of Mark underlined, but you ought to underline in purple ink where it says *"And when ye stand praying, forgive."* That ought to be foremost in your mind, your heart, and your spirit. Without forgiveness it is impossible to make your faith work.

The person who wronged you has to answer to God. You don't answer for him or her; you answer for *you*. The only thing you can do for them is forgive them, pray for them, and go on. You control you.

If you want strong faith, learn how to forgive when you stand praying.